Sound familiar?

That's because loads of people think that way - but when you're already feeling pretty bad, thoughts like these make you feel even worse.

The fact is, certain thoughts **cause** bad feelings. It's not just the other way round. So one way to feel better is to respond differently to upsetting thoughts.

This book will show you how.

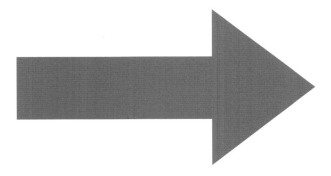

Turn the page and you'll see what we mean.

GOOD MOVE!

You turned the page!

You didn't say "Oh, forget it!" and chuck the book out of the window. You turned the page and took a giant leap towards feeling better - by yourself.

Keep on turning and you'll find out how to *keep on* feeling better and better, with the

Amazing Unhelpful Thought Busting Programme

Now you're going to learn to spot some unhelpful thoughts.

LET'S PLAY DETECTIVE

Magnifying Glass at the ready?

The key to good detective work is to slow things down and be on the lookout.

Try this task to start noticing your own unhelpful thoughts.

Imagine yourself into each situation, and try to spot the thoughts that pop into your mind.

1). You're late for an important meeting. You're stuck in traffic and can see the building you want to reach. You know you're going to be really late.

2). You invite friends round for a meal, but notice one of them doesn't eat much of it and says they're not hungry.

3). You play sport but this week you're not picked to play.

Then complete the worksheet on pages 8-9. Use the questions to help you identify the thoughts that occur. Write down as many as you notice, then turn the page to label the thoughts.

My Unhelpful Thoughts

Noticing thoughts that have a bad impact on how you feel and what you do.

How to fill in this sheet

Choose a time when you felt worse. What went through your mind at the time?

- About what you've done or not done?
- About you?
- About others?
- About what has happened?
- About what might happen?
- About what others think about you?
- Any pictures or images that come into your mind?

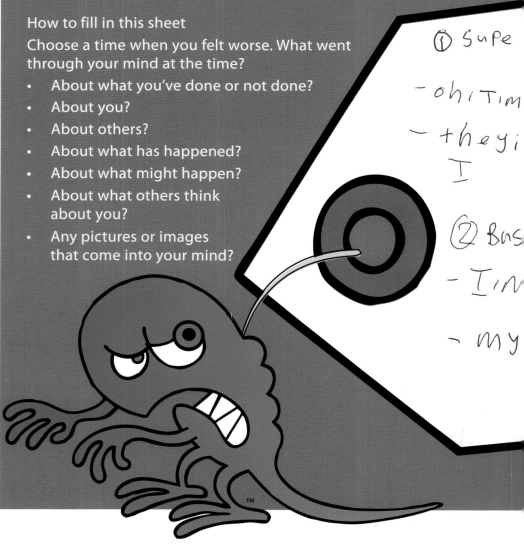

rket

aking too larg.

very rude

ave to Rush now

No show

going to be late

whale day is Ruined

living
life to
the full
www.llttf.com

Unhelpful Thinking Styles

We can fall into upsetting habits of thinking called unhelpful thinking styles. They are habits of thinking we can fall into time and time again. These thoughts are important because:

- they worsen how we feel emotionally and physically
- they affect what we do. So, we might say no to something when yes could be fun.

This unhelpful thought spotter will help you spot when your thinking isn't helping. Look back at the thoughts you wrote down on the last page. Now label them using the unhelpful thought spotter here.

Are any of these thinking styles familiar? Have you been here before?

If you tick one or more boxes, you've spotted an unhelpful thought that you can aim to change.

Are you your own worst critic?

Do you always seem to be beating yourself up about something?

Do you focus on the bad stuff?

As if you were looking at the world through darkened glasses?

Do you have a gloomy view of the future?

Expecting everything to turn out badly?

Are you jumping to the worst conclusions?

Thinking it's the end of the world.

Do you assume that others see you badly?

When you haven't checked whether it's true, it's called 'Mind Reading'

Do you take responsibility for everything?

Including things that aren't your fault?

Are you always saying things like 'should' and 'got to'?

Setting impossible standards for yourself?

Turn the page to respond differently

The Amazing Unhelpful Thought Busting Programme

Step 1

First, label the thought

When you notice an unhelpful thought that has a bad impact on how you feel or what you do, don't get caught up in it. Instead, just mentally step back and stick a label on it.

"Oh that's just one of those unhelpful thoughts".

When you label a thought this way, **it** loses its power and **you** realise it's just part of being upset.

It's not the truth, it's just one of those unhelpful thoughts.

You could even talk to it. Say: "You're spotted! I'm not playing that game again!"

Turn over for **Step 2**

The Amazing Unhelpful Thought Busting Programme

Step 2

NOW LEAVE IT ALONE

Mentally turn your back on the thought. Don't challenge it or try to argue with it, just let it be.

Unhelpful thoughts love attention so don't give them any.

Instead, think about what you're doing right now, or stuff that you're planning for the future, or things you've achieved lately.

Step 3 next

The Amazing Unhelpful Thought Busting Programme

Step 3

STAND UP TO IT!

Don't be bossed about by unhelpful thoughts

Unhelpful thoughts can be intimidating. But although they sound strong, really they're weak underneath. And they tell lies.

They say you won't like doing something. They say you'll fail if you try. They tell you you're rubbish or you're scared or nobody likes you.

Just because the thought claims something doesn't mean it's true.

Act against it and test it out!
If the thought says "Don't" then DO!
If the thought says "Can't" say "CAN!"
Right back at it.

Easy for us to say? You're right.

But if you don't give it a try you'll never know.

Turn over for the next step

17

Step 4

GIVE YOURSELF A BREAK

Be a better friend to yourself, you deserve it.

Unhelpful thoughts are how we beat ourselves up when we're upset. We often say things to ourselves that are critical and nasty – things we would never say to someone we cared for. And we often say things to ourselves in such a nasty or scary tone.

So if you're having trouble with an upsetting thought, think what a person who really loved and wanted the best for you would say. What words of encouragement and support might they offer?

They'd disagree with the unhelpful thoughts. They'd remind you that you're not rubbish, or stupid, or bound to fail.

Trust these compassionate things and let them help you get rid of the unhelpful thoughts.

Turn over for **Step 5**

HOW TO BEAT THE REALLY BAD ONES

Some unhelpful thoughts are hard to beat.

They keep coming back and you wonder if you'll ever get the better of them.

Here are three things you can do that will help.

Look at the situation differently

First, imagine what it would be like if it was a friend, not you, who was having this thought. What advice would you give? Now give the same advice to yourself.

Put your thought or worry into perspective. Will it matter in six weeks or six months? Will you even remember what the problem was? If it won't matter then, it's probably not that important now.

How would others deal with the problem? Think about someone who seems to handle problems well and work out what they would do, or how they would think in this situation.

Really Unhelpful Thought

Turn over to **RECAP**

The Amazing Unhelpful Thought Busting Programme

Recap

SO:

The Amazing Unhelpful Thought Busting Programme

Unhelpful thoughts mess you up and actually **cause** bad feelings. Beat those thoughts and you'll feel better. When you notice an upsetting thought:

1. LABEL IT

Oh, you're just one of those unhelpful thoughts.

2. LEAVE IT

Unhelpful thoughts need attention, so don't give them any.

3. STAND UP TO IT

Unhelpful thoughts can be scary and intimidating, but tell lies. You can beat them.

4. GIVE YOURSELF A BREAK

What would someone who really loved you say? Trust them and let them help you beat the unhelpful thought.

5. LOOK AT IT DIFFERENTLY

Give yourself the advice you'd give to a friend. Ask yourself if it will matter in six weeks or six months. Pick someone you you trust and respect and work out how they would handle the situation.

So what are you waiting for? Let's try it out

living
life to
the full
www.llttf.com

The Amazing Unhelpful Thought Busting Programme

Try the Amazing Unhelpful Thought Busting Programme (AUTBP) - for unhelpful thoughts that have a bad impact on how you feel emotionally or physically or what you do.

1 Label it
- Oh, you're just one of those unhelpful thoughts.

2 Leave it
- Unhelpful thoughts often demand attention. Let them be.

3 Stand up to it
- Unhelpful thoughts can be intimidating. You can beat them.

4 Be kind to yourself: Give yourself a break

- What warm words of encouragement would someone say?
  Say them to yourself.

5 Look at it differently

- Give yourself the advice you'd give a friend.

- Ask yourself if it will matter in six weeks or months?

- What would other people you trust and respect say?

- Does it really matter so much?

- Are you looking at the whole picture?

GO
FOR
IT!

Don't worry

If this seems hard at first. A good place to start is to practice on unhelpful thoughts that are only slightly upsetting to begin with.

It takes practice to beat upsetting thoughts.

But the Amazing Unhelpful Thought Busting Program really works, so keep trying and within a few days, you'll have your unhelpful thoughts on the run and be feeling better.

Remember the key thing is to plan to practice this approach.

Use the Planner sheet on the next two pages to create a good plan.

living
life to
the full
www.llttf.com

Planner Sheet

Make a Plan!

1. What am I going to do?

Just one small thing

2. When am I going to do it?

That way you'll know if you don't do it

3. What problems or difficulties could arise, and how can I overcome them?

4. Is my planned task -

	Yes	No
• Useful for understanding or changing how I am?	☐	☐
• Specific, so that I will know when I have done it?	☐	☐
• Realistic, practical and achievable?	☐	☐

My notes:

WHERE TO GET EVEN MORE ADVICE AND SUPPORT

Sometimes, unhelpful thoughts feel like part of you and you just can't seem to label them, leave them or stand up to them.

That's when you need a bit more advice and support than this little book can give.

You can also get it at **www.llttf.com** - the award-winning web course. It's also the most recommended online resource for anxiety and depression by NHS England.*

This little book is a companion to all the one's on the right. When you've sorted your current problem, you might want to choose another little book and work on something else in your life.

*Bennion et al, 2017. BMJ Open http://bmjopen.bmj.com/content/7/1/e014844

Look out for more resources like this

Order them at www.llttf.com/shop
Or visit www.llttf.com/ebooks for links to
Kindle and Apple ibook versions.

Acknowledgements: We wish to thank Realspeak and the LLTTF team for their help with design and content. Philip Munro for the illustrations and Tara Surr for typesetting. The terms Five Areas, LLTTF and the Bad thought bug are registered trademarks of Five Areas Resources Ltd.

*Darton, Longman and Todd edition.

Over 1,500,000 LLTTF books in print

What we think can affect how we feel and what we do. At times of distress it's common for us to fall into habits of unhelpful thinking. These thoughts cause us to feel bad, and react in ways that worsen how we feel. Based on the popular cognitive behavioural therapy (CBT) approach this powerful little book will help you respond differently to unhelpful thoughts.

About the Author

Dr Chris Williams is Emeritus Professor of Psychosocial Psychiatry at the University of Glasgow, Scotland, UK and a Fellow of the Royal College of Psychiatrists. His main clinical and research interest is in the evaluation of educational self-help approaches based on the cognitive behavioural therapy (CBT) approach. He has developed various written and computer-based educational self-help resources for low mood, stress and eating problems, and has twice been President of the British Association for Behavioural and Cognitive Psychotherapies - the lead body for CBT in the United Kingdom. He is Patron of the charity Triumph over Phobia and a Medical adviser to Anxiety UK. Dr Williams is also Director of Five Areas Ltd which publishes this book and a range of other wellbeing resources. He is an award winning author and his books and websites are widely used in the UK, Ireland and North America.

Helping you help yourself www.llttf.com
Supporter/Practitioner resource site www.fiveareas.com
Buy books, courses and other resources www.llttf.com/shop
Also available on Kindle and as Apple ibooks
(www.llttf.com/ebooks)

Published by Five Areas Ltd.
Copyright © Five Areas Resources Limited (2020)
All rights reserved. First Published 2007.
Second edition 2014. Third edition 2017.
This Fourth edition 2020.

ISBN: 978-1-906564-74-2

For members of the public, supporters and practitioners:

 www.llttf.com/facebook

 @llttfnews

 Supporter and practitioner training at www.fiveareas.com/training

9 781906 564742

Home Fires:
20 poems 4 2012

Boni Sones OBE

New works for The Jubilee and
London 2012 Olympics